THOMAS AQUINAS

A Life from Beginning to End

Copyright © 2020 by Hourly History.

Table of Contents

Introduction

Thomas Aquinas was a rare breed of theologian; he dared to venture into philosophical quandaries that many of the traditionalists feared to tread. After taking a vow of chastity and poverty, Aquinas's greatest desire was to contemplate God and creation, two things that he did with exquisite erudition.

His critics sometimes lambasted him as being nothing more than an "intellectual beggar," but even amid the harshest attacks on both his faith and his character, Aquinas was always more than up for the challenge and ready to deliver a counter-attack whether in public debate or in the form of a written theological treatise on the subject. Thomas Aquinas never shied away from a fight and was always eager to delve into even the most complex of theological arguments.

Indeed, even as a youngster when he attended his first form of formal education at the Abbey of Monte Cassino, he was noted for frequently asking his superiors, "What is God?" Such a basic yet awe-inspiring question was something that most never even thought to ask or were too afraid to question. Thomas Aquinas had neither of these problems. For him, it was only natural to prove the fundamental tenants of creation. It was not a sign of lack of faith; on the contrary, it was indicative that he longed to get closer to both creation and the creator by coming to a greater understanding of them both. As you read this book, you will find that this desire for greater understanding of the divine was indeed the driving force behind the life of Thomas Aquinas.

Chapter One

Born into a Noble Family

"One will observe that all things are arranged according to their degrees of beauty and excellence, and that the nearer they are to God, the more beautiful and better they are."

—Thomas Aquinas

For someone who would later be known for his vows of poverty and simplistic, monkish existence, Thomas Aquinas had some not so humble beginnings. He was born in 1225, and his name stems from the place of his birth in the auspices of the castle of Roccasecca, Aquino, in the Kingdom of Sicily (present-day Italian region of Lazio).

His father was a nobleman by the name of Landulf, who served at the court of King Roger II as a knight. His mother, Theodora, hailed from Naples in southwestern Italy. On his father's side of the family, there was a long tradition of military service, with the one exception being that of Thomas's uncle Sinibald who served as an abbot at the first Benedictine monastery. It was the template established by his uncle Sinibald upon which Thomas would eventually mold his career. If legend is to be believed, Thomas's life trajectory was aiming in this direction even before he was born. His mother Theodora allegedly had a holy hermit—a kind of religious, roving vagabond—prophecy over her unborn child, saying that one day he "would enter the Order of Friars."

This was a career which began in earnest at the tender age of five when Thomas began his formal education at the monastery of Monte Cassino. Here, he first mastered the basics of his craft, and he would remain on at the school until he was 13 years of age. Not a whole lot is known about Thomas's early years, but during his tenure at Monte Cassino, he was most remembered for his early budding philosophical thought, such as the time he boldly asked the question, "What is God?"

Aquinas's stint at Monte Cassino came to an abrupt end, however, when the political situation in the region became quite untenable. By 1239, Emperor Frederick II of the Holy Roman Empire was embroiled in a feud with the then-reigning pope, Gregory IX. In the past few years, Frederick had been on a campaign of expansion that included taking over additional parts of Italy—a conquest in which his troops were not at all hesitant to lay siege to monasteries and even hospitals in their mission to expand the Empire. Although the Vatican was supposed to be an ally of the Holy Roman Empire, these misadventures right in the pope's backyard did not sit well with him at all.

In light of these circumstances, Frederick II was excommunicated from the Catholic Church for the third time in 1239. If the pope thought that excommunicating the most powerful leader in his vicinity would bring peace, however, he was gravely mistaken, and the conflict continued. Due to this instability, Thomas Aquinas was sent off to his mother's hometown of Naples, where he would go to school at the *studium generale*, a university that had recently been established by Frederick II.

The coursework that Aquinas was immersed in at the university included all the classic works of the great philosophers, such as Maimonides, Averroes, and Aristotle, but most important to him during this time was the living breathing example of the Dominican monks that he encountered. Aquinas was inspired by the monks' vows of poverty and that they eschewed the things of this world in order to exert all of their energy toward getting closer to God.

Some turned their noses at these poverty-stricken monks, likening them to nothing more than intellectual beggars. But in them, Aquinas thought he saw kindred spirits. He longed to don their cassock and join them in their pursuit of higher knowledge. Gazing at these wizened old spiritual scholars, he felt that he had found his true calling in life, but he would soon also find no small amount of disapproval and bitter resentment from his family.

Chapter Two

Aquinas at the University of Naples

"There is nothing on this Earth more to be prized than true friendship."

—Thomas Aquinas

Although Thomas Aquinas studied under the auspices of great teachers at the University of Naples, he was apparently surrounded by all manner of vice. He would later describe that it was "a very paradise of God, but inhabited by demons." During this time in which he was ensconced in a citadel of God surrounded by a region of worldly influence, Aquinas likened himself to Daniel being held captive in Babylon, and he prayed to be "kept clean."

It was here that Thomas came under the tutelage of a professor who was known as Peter of Ireland. Not a whole lot is known about this mysterious Peter of Ireland, but later research has uncovered that he was most likely a Benedictine monk referred to as Petrus de Donis who lived and worked in the region at the time. Peter is said to have lectured on the subjects of rhetoric and humanities.

Although many things in Thomas Aquinas's early life remain a question mark to the reader of modern events, one thing seems to be clear: he was an avid pupil from the very beginning of his formal education. Aquinas would eschew childhood activities that other youth enjoyed in favor of the solitude of his books and his studies. It is said that he became such a rapid learner that soon he was repeating the lectures his professors gave to him nearly verbatim. This earned Aquinas the reputation of being brilliant. Another thing that he gained a reputation for was his acts of charitable giving. Aquinas did indeed come from a rather wealthy family, yet he never used his money for his own luxury; instead, he could be often seen giving alms to the poor. This was apparently a tradition that began very early in his life.

As a boy, Aquinas had become fascinated with handing out money to the begging passers-by that he came across. According to legend, his father chastised him for giving too much, but that didn't stop young Thomas. On one occasion, he allegedly stuffed food in his coat and went out to give it to the poor. His father stopped him in his tracks and asked him, "What do you have there?" Thomas then let the items drop when they supposedly transformed into roses and fell at his feet. However this mysterious transmutation of bread to roses may have occurred, his father apparently took it as a miracle and never bothered the youth again about his exuberant giving. But even though he now had his family's tacit approval for his almsgiving, it is said that Thomas, wishing to be humble, continued to give to the poor in stealth, lest he draw unwanted attention to his giving. Nevertheless, he soon became known as a very charitable young man.

Toward the end of his time at the university, Aquinas developed a keen interest in the local Dominican friars of

Naples. He began to incessantly ask his teachers to allow him to visit them at their monastery. His instructors allowed him to indulge himself in these visits, but it is said that they never imagined that someone of such a high-ranking family on the social ladder would actually aspire to become a poverty-stricken friar themselves. They believed that it was nothing more than a passing fancy and had no idea how mistaken they were.

Chapter Three

Joining the Dominican Friars

"The things that we love tell us what we are."

—Thomas Aquinas

Thomas was barely 18 years of age when he decided that he would like to spend the rest of his life in the monkish habits of a Dominican friar. He aspired to be like such saintly and impoverished figures as Saint Francis of Assisi, who had died a year after Thomas was born. The actual Order of Dominicans had only been established some ten years before that, but by the time Aquinas was reaching adulthood, their fame for faith, devotion, and austerity had already spread far and wide.

As esteemed as these monks were for their efforts, a life of poverty was not what was expected of a scion of such wealth and nobility as Thomas Aquinas. As such, as soon as word got back to his father of his plans, he issued Aquinas an ultimatum in no uncertain terms that he was to abandon any plans of joining the Dominicans. Not only that, but he also issued a warning to the monastery itself, telling the Dominican Fathers that if they were to so much as think about accepting Thomas Aquinas into their fold, he would make sure that they would have the full wrath of the

Holy Roman emperor come down upon them. This must have given them some pause, but these were men of faith after all, and if they felt that Aquinas had a God-given calling to join their ranks, they were not going to let threats—even from the emperor—sway them in their decision making.

According to legend, it was allegedly a miraculous sign that convinced the friars that it was indeed God's will for Thomas Aquinas to join them. It is claimed that one day while Thomas was praying, the monks observed his countenance suddenly supernaturally glow with the "blessed light of the glory of God." It was allegedly this bright shining halo over Aquinas's head that led the order to openly defy the threats of Aquinas's father and allow him to join their ranks. As such, in the late summer month of August in 1243, Thomas received the white robes of a Dominican initiate without delay.

Although the monks made the claim that these events were God's will, there were still many detractors from Aquinas's family. They charged the monks with nothing short of manipulation in their efforts to get Thomas to join their flock. Aquinas's mother too, who although is said to have encouraged much of her son's piety early on, was deeply disappointed in his decision to join the monks. She expected great things for her son, and him being buried in the living tomb of a Dominican monastery was not among her ideas of future greatness. She was so dismayed, in fact, that she set off on a journey to Naples to intercept her son in an effort to change his mind.

Thomas Aquinas was tipped off to this fact, however, and decided to skip town in order to avoid his meddling mother. As soon as he got permission from his instructors, he left for Rome and was sure to take a road that he knew his mother would not. It was after going down this road less traveled that Aquinas made his way to the Roman convent of Santa Sabina. Here, he sought to hide until the storm of his family's wrath and discontent blew over. His mother quickly learned of his plans, however, and raced off to Santa Sabina. It is said that she banged upon the gates of the abbey, demanding to have an audience with her son.

It must have been quite a spectacle to see this noblewoman and her entourage camped out around this modest monastery. Yet it was all to no avail since Aquinas had expressly informed the church officials that he was not to be disturbed by anyone—not even his own mother. Denied access to her son, Theodora had no choice but to march back home, empty-handed and broken-hearted.

Chapter Four

Kidnapped and Imprisoned

"To one who has faith, no explanation is necessary. To one without faith, no explanation is possible."

—Thomas Aquinas

When Aquinas's mother Theodora learned that she would not be able to see her son, she sought a higher authority—Pope Innocent IV. The Dominicans, fearing papal interference, quickly decided to send Aquinas off to Paris so that he could avoid the reach of the pope. He left for Paris in the company of four of his fellow monks from the monastery, traveling through backroads in the hope of giving the papacy the slip.

In this secretive entourage, Aquinas made it all the way to Tuscany before they were finally intercepted. His group was surrounded by a band of armed men, and Aquinas was promptly taken into their custody. He was then whisked away to his parents' estate at Roccasecca. It is said that his teary-eyed mother was the first to greet him. Past biographers have reflected over whether these tears were remorse for the state in which her son had been returned to her, or over her sadness to know that he was firmly fixed against what she had planned for his life. At any rate, no matter how much she tried to assuage Aquinas's ire at being accosted, or attempted to reason with him over the direction he should take in life, Aquinas refused to listen.

Shockingly enough, after finding that her son would not hear her out, Theodora decided to put him under a kind of house arrest by having him locked up in a tower of the family castle. Here, Aquinas would remain for the better part of a year as his mother and other relatives continued their petitions to make him change his mind. They insisted that Aquinas should not demean himself by becoming what amounted to an intellectual beggar living with a bunch of poverty-stricken monks.

Whatever argument that was brought to Aquinas as to why he should cease and desist, he was always able to turn it on its head and argue right back that they should not be so basely interfering with what God had ordained for him to do. If they thought that kidnapping him and locking him up in a tower could dissuade him, they were most certainly mistaken. The more they sought to pull him back from the Dominicans, the more it pushed him further into their embrace.

With the family growing desperate and fearing the growing spectacle of what their neighbors might think to find that they had imprisoned one of their own members, Aquinas's brothers Landulf and Ronald were next in line to try to dissuade him. Unlike Theodora's, their efforts amounted to more or less harassment, even on one occasion physically ripping off his monkish robe and forcing him to put on the civilian attire they had brought up to the tower. Their efforts grew much more devious even than this, and when they realized that their pious brother was too dedicated to God to listen to their arguments, they plotted to make him a little less pious.

Landulf and Ronald reportedly thought that if they could make their brother step out of his world of faith and prayer and into one of sinful indulgence, they would be able to make him forget all about his monkish fantasy. It was with this in mind that they concocted a scheme to lock their brother up with a prostitute. As bizarre as it may sound, they acquired the services of a beautiful young woman, who was apparently well-versed in the things of the flesh. The brothers shut her in Aquinas's room in the tower, locking the two up together.

Aquinas would later recall that he was indeed attracted to the woman but, knowing exactly what his brothers were up to and what the loss of his chastity might mean for his monkish vows, he cast out his lust and aggressively pushed the woman away. According to Aquinas's later recollection, he took a "burning brand out of the fire" and "chased the temptress from his presence." It is said that after he wielded the flaming brand at the woman, Aquinas took it and made the sign of the cross on the wall before falling upon his knees and thanking God for allowing him to prevail against temptation. After praying in this fashion, it is said that Aquinas fell into a deep sleep. According to legend, he then witnessed two angels.

The angels allegedly wrapped a cord around his waist and told him, "We come to thee from God to give thee the grace of everlasting virginity." This was apparently not an easy designation to be given, because Aquinas would later recollect that as soon as the angels had tied the cord around his waist, he screamed out loud in pain. The sound caused the men standing watch outside his room to check on him to make sure that he was alright. Aquinas told them that he was fine and went back to his blissful sleep.

It was claimed that the cord was indeed real, and Aquinas would carry an approximation of it for the rest of his life, later attesting that "many miracles were worked by it." At any rate, it is said that as word of the imprisonment of Thomas Aquinas grew, none other than the pope himself warned the family to set him free at once. And so, Aquinas was freed from his bonds and allowed to return to the life of chastity and austerity that he had chosen.

Chapter Five

Journey to Cologne

"To bear with patience wrongs done to oneself is a mark of perfection, but to bear with patience wrongs done to someone else is a mark of actual sin."

—Thomas Aquinas

The family had been put on notice that they should set Aquinas free, but even after one year of imprisonment, it was a tough pill for them to swallow. In order to save face and avoid the embarrassment that his internment engendered, they reportedly devised a plan to make it seem as if he had escaped from their clutches instead.

Like some scene right out of the Bible, Aquinas's sisters lowered him down from his room in the tower by a basket, which was received by Aquinas's fellow Dominican monks who were patiently waiting outside. Aquinas was 19 years of age when he reclaimed this freedom of body, spirit, and destiny.

Although his family had freed him from his constraints, they had not yet entirely ceased in their efforts to dissuade him from his course in life, as was evidenced when they personally requested for Pope Innocent to annul his profession. But the pope, who had previously criticized the family for confining the boy, was not about to suddenly chastise his desire to be a monk without further information about it. In 1244, the pope summoned Thomas Aquinas to the Vatican so that he could talk to the young man in person. It is said by later chroniclers that here Aquinas put up such a spirited defense of his decision to become a monk that no one could doubt that it was from God.

Nevertheless, the pope, feeling the need to assuage the notable family from which Aquinas hailed, attempted to convince Aquinas to sign on with the more respectable (by the standards of the time) Abbey of Monte Cassino rather than the austere and bleak environs of a Benedictine monastery. This would provide Aquinas the eventual role as abbot, giving him an important position of theological prestige along with the temporal esteem of having a substantial income for taking on the post. The pope figured that this would be much easier for Aquinas's family to accept and live with than the idea of him becoming a poor beggar of a monk shut up in a monastery.

Still, even after the pope attempted to persuade him to concede to this one adjustment of his destiny, Aquinas remained steadfast and would not turn away from what he believed to be his true mission. Pope Innocent, realizing that Aquinas would not bend, acquiesced and named him as an official friar of Mary, which was another way of calling him a Dominican in the common parlance of the day.

Shortly after this confirmation was made, Thomas Aquinas made the acquaintance of John the Teuton, who was the master general of the Dominican Order at the time. John took Aquinas under his wing and sent him to Cologne so that he could be educated under the auspices of the theologian known as Albertus Magnus, or as he has later been referred in the annals of Catholic history, Saint Albert the Great. Albert was a leading religious scholar in his day and among the first to entertain the writings of the Ancient Greek philosopher Aristotle.

Even though the nation of Germany as we know it today did not exist yet, Cologne of Thomas Aquinas's time had deep German roots all the same. With its thinly spaced avenues and shops on every corner, German industry and ingenuity seemed to be already busting at the seams. Although he was a new addition, it is said that it wasn't long before Aquinas's peers realized that he was a serious student of the faith. They also noticed that he was an incredibly quiet student as well. This served as a source of ridicule for his detractors that lambasted him as a sullen outsider and even coined a nickname which mocked his Italian heritage: "dumb Sicilian ox."

Aquinas was indeed rather quiet when he first arrived in Cologne, and some chose to interpret his silence as stupidity by joking that he was a "mute ox," but these crude remarks were soon proven entirely false. Soon Albert was having Aquinas publicly defend complex theological arguments in front of all of his fellow pupils, demonstrating just how vast his understanding and erudition was.

When Thomas Aquinas publicly broke his silence in this manner, even those who had initially met him with mockery and jeers had to agree—dumb ox he most certainly was not. This point was proudly proclaimed by Albert as well, who is said to have declared of Aquinas, "We have called him the dumb ox, but he will bellow so loud that the sound of his voice will be heard throughout the whole world."

Chapter Six

The Execution of His Brother

"Idleness is the hook with which the devil fishes, with which all bait is taken."

—Thomas Aquinas

Aquinas was in his early twenties when he began to truly come into his own under the guidance of Albert in Cologne. Albert began to count Aquinas as his number one protégé and as such was inclined to take him with him during all of his subsequent travels, as was the case when Albert took Thomas with him to Paris in order to continue his studies at the Dominican Convent of St. James.

Here, it is said that Aquinas really buckled down with his theological learning, reading Scripture night and day as well as further studying the works of the ancient Greek philosopher Aristotle. Although Aristotle was certainly not a Christian, many Christians of Aquinas's day had begun to open up to Aristotle, valuing his treatises on logic and reason and framing them within a Christian worldview.

It was also during his stay in Paris that Thomas Aquinas met Giovanni di Fidanza, or as he became known, Saint Bonaventure. Like many of his contemporaries, Bonaventure was impressed with the devotion that young

Aquinas displayed. He took note of his studious bent and dedication to learning. At one point, it is said that when Bonaventure was in the midst of writing a biography of Saint Francis of Assisi, Aquinas announced to his fellow book writer, "Let us leave a saint to write the life of a saint."

So it was that Aquinas was ushered in as a great teacher of the faith, and in Paris, he would indeed teach for the better part of two years. After this, he returned to Cologne with Albert, making the journey on foot just as he had arrived. Upon his return, it is said that Aquinas began to gain quite a wide following, larger than was the case before he had left. So great was his draw that the attendance of the courses he taught was soon greater than that of Albert himself. This is the moment they say that Thomas Aquinas began to surpass his mentor. This was a point in Aquinas's life when he also became increasingly prolific in writing the philosophical works for which he would become so famous later on. In general, this was a time in which the passion of Thomas Aquinas seemed to burn the brightest.

Those graced with his presence were said to have been infused with the "ardour of the love of God which burned in his soul." But ardor or not, the political situation would take another hit when Frederick II was yet again excommunicated at the Council of Lyons on July 17, 1245. These were indeed perilous times to be catholic, and Aquinas's own family found themselves having to choose between their spiritual benefactor the pope or their temporal, yet more immediate benefactor, Emperor Frederick II.

In a move that must have made Thomas Aquinas proud, his family put their earthly land holdings aside and in the course of the conflict ended up siding with the pope rather than Emperor Frederick. In this switching of allegiance, it appears that Thomas's brother Ronald was the most dedicated because shortly thereafter, he had joined up with a group of conspirators to plot against the emperor. This scheme was soon uncovered, however, and Ronald was arrested and charged with treason, resulting in his prompt conviction and execution in 1246.

If the execution of Ronald was not a clear enough sign that the Aquinas family was on the outs with the Holy Roman emperor, events in 1250 would bring it all home when the emperor besieged the family castle in Roccasecca. After the smoke cleared, the family had become more aligned with the Vatican than ever, and Aquinas's sister even became an abbess at a Benedictine convent shortly thereafter.

Yet the greatest calamity to face Aquinas wouldn't come from outside forces but rather from within his own faith. At the University of Paris, there was a certain religious guru by the name of William of Saint-Amour who began to openly speak out against Thomas Aquinas and the Dominican friars. William apparently was upset that Aquinas had recently been drawing away much of his congregants with his words of theological wisdom. Angered by what he perceived as an affront, William set about writing a book that disparaged the order to which Aquinas belonged.

Called *On the Dangers of the Final Days*, the book's main theme was borrowed from the writings of the Apostle

Paul who said, "In the last days perilous times shall come. For men shall be lovers of their own selves, covetous, boasters, proud, blasphemers, disobedient to parents, unthankful, unholy." This verse was widely taken as a warning to beware of pompous and ego-driven preachers leading the flock astray, and William masterfully applied it to the orders of Franciscans and Dominicans. By doing so, he insinuated that Thomas Aquinas was one of these treacherous teachers. William claimed that much of the calamities of the times were in fact due to the embrace of false doctrines, such as those the Franciscans and Dominicans espoused.

Among other things, the book criticized the main foundation with which the monks of these orders gained their sustenance. In those days, both the Franciscans and Dominicans basically lived as beggars, living off whatever donations and alms they were provided by generous givers. Other more established orders had their own sources of revenue through the property that they held and other pastoral benefices, such as being paid to copy manuscripts and other routine work. The book lambasted the Franciscans and Dominicans beggarly ways as being a lazy affront and claimed that they leeched off others with no theological justification in doing so.

Aquinas and those like him were also roundly criticized for relying too heavily on the philosopher Aristotle, who was believed to have been an atheist and who believed the universe had no beginning and no creator. Such belief would indeed be contrary to Scripture which has God stating, "I am the beginning and the end."

Thomas Aquinas had an interesting solution to these theological problems, but his solution would only bring him more criticism. When it came to the ultimate nature of the universe, some would even go so far as to say that Aquinas had developed an outlook that was panentheistic in nature. As Aquinas himself was more likely to describe it, he had an all-in-God interpretation of creation. This is sort of a reverse take on the classical pantheistic notion that every living thing is a small manifestation of God. The subtle difference was that Aquinas believed that while the divine was present in all things, it was not so much that all matter was a manifestation of God, but that God was somehow present in all matter.

Aquinas believed that this divine spark was present throughout all creation, but humanity had a very special dose of this divinity in the form of the Holy Spirit. He believed that every human had this essence within them, but not every human had been enlightened to reach inward and tap into it. Aquinas would eventually crystalize these conclusions in his famous *Summa theologiae*.

Although this philosophical framework would be the platform of one of his major works, it would also lead those that disagreed with it to condemn him as a false teacher or otherwise heretical to the faith. Aquinas initially responded to these attacks by the best way he knew—by writing a book of counter-arguments against his detractors. In the aptly named *Against Those Who Assail the Worship of God and Religion*, he laid out the defense of both himself and his fellow brothers in the faith. Initially this book only seemed to provide even more fuel to the fire, and these contrary camps of theologians continued to spar back and forth.

Nevertheless, as many critics as he may have had, Aquinas had some pretty powerful supporters as well. On the official level, the school authorities came out against William's book and attempted to vindicate both Thomas Aquinas and the Franciscan and Dominican orders from the slander that his book contained. These efforts proved to be too little too late, however, and once the general body had read William's book, many had already made up their mind to entertain the type of criticism and theories that the work contained.

As a result of all the attacks thrown his way, Thomas Aquinas would soon find himself in the greatest ethical challenge of his life. His closely cherished ideals were under siege, but the man who was being ridiculed as nothing more than a monkish beggar had chosen to fight.

Chapter Seven

Skeptics and Believers

"I cannot understand how anyone who knows he is in a state of mortal sin can laugh or be merry."

—Thomas Aquinas

In the midst of the controversy created by William, Thomas Aquinas had been called upon as an apologist for the Franciscans and Dominicans. Wasting no time, Thomas appeared before a group of assembled theologians of all stripes and made his case. It is said that in doing so, he pleaded the cause of the mendicant orders with such ease that he immediately won over the pope, who officially condemned the work of William of Saint-Amour in October of 1256.

With the future of the orders more secure than ever, Thomas would be recalled to France before the year was out. He left Italy by boat, hoping to make a much faster trip than he would have made on foot. Yet in those days, seaborn travel—although faster—was rife with danger, and this particular trip proved to be full of hardship. The weather, which was calm when they left, quickly took a turn for the worse. Aquinas, fearing that the ship would capsize, is said to have engaged in intense prayer until the ship was able to right itself and arrive at its destination.

Upon his return to Paris, Aquinas was pressured to study for his doctor's degree as soon as possible, but not everyone was willing to forget about the recent theological turmoil that had swirled around him. It was only with the pope on his side, who is said to have issued nothing short of eleven bulls or papal proclamations demanding that Aquinas be allowed to proceed, that his path was made clear.

Despite these efforts made on his behalf, it was Aquinas's own self-doubt that hampered his progress the most. In many ways, he questioned whether or not he was worthy of the role that he had been given, and he often doubted that he would be able to succeed. According to legend, Aquinas was in such a cloud of despair and doubt that when he fell asleep on the evening before he was to present himself before the examiners, he cried out to God in prayer, expressing his distress. Similar to when he was locked up in the tower of his family's castle, it is said that Thomas Aquinas fell asleep while he prayed.

In his dreams, he apparently had a vision of Saint Dominic, the founder of his order, sent from heaven to console him in the midst of his turmoil. The figure is said to have inquired Aquinas, "Why do you thus pray to God in tears?" to which Thomas duly answered, "Because the burden of the Doctorate, for which my knowledge is not sufficient, is laid upon me, and also because I do not know which text to choose for my discourse." After expressing these doubts, Saint Dominic is said to have assured him, "Behold thou art heard; take the burden of the Doctorate upon thee, for God is with thee." Aquinas awoke shortly thereafter and felt as if he were indeed imbued with a supernatural sense of self-confidence and emboldened for the task which was at hand.

In late October of 1257, Aquinas was indeed made an official doctor of the faith. From here on out, he entered into a period of voluminous writing in which he created great masterpieces such as the epic *Summa contra Gentiles*. In this piece, Aquinas sought to build a bridge between Greek and Arab thought that had filtered into Western Europe by framing it into a Christian perspective. His main argument was that the highly intelligent thought of non-Christians shined even brighter when placed under the light of the Christian faith. In other words, rather than shy away from the advances of non-Christians, they should be incorporated as wayward divine sparks that need to be brought back under Christian dominion.

Right around this time, Aquinas was also working on a treatise on the Epistles of St. Paul. Incredibly enough, Aquinas would claim that none other than Paul himself would come down to him in a vision to express his approval for what he had written. Still, this pales in comparison to the claim he made shortly after this supposed vision of the Apostle Paul because this vision is said to have been followed by an encore supernatural visitation with Jesus Christ. According to legend, not only did Thomas Aquinas have an audience with Christ, but several of his fellow monks bore witness to the encounter as well.

Although most would agree that these fantastical tales are merely allegories, there are those that believe the accounts occurred just as they were described. It seems that just as was the case during the times in which he lived,

Thomas Aquinas was quite good at provoking both skeptics and believers alike.

Chapter Eight

The Errors of the Greeks

"The prayerless soul advances in nothing."

—Thomas Aquinas

Even while hammering out his masterworks, from the outset of the 1260s, Thomas Aquinas was a man on the move. In 1261, Aquinas was summoned by none other than Pope Urban IV. The new pope wished to finally put an end to much of the strife that marked the reign of his predecessor, and it was the wisdom of Thomas Aquinas that he sought most in order to help him mend rent theological fences.

One of the greatest of these theological tears was one that predated even the previous pope: The Great Schism between the western and eastern Catholic churches. The east, largely composed of Greek-speaking peoples, had fallen out with their Latin-based brethren in the west. They had become known as the Greek Orthodox Faith and were considered heretical by the Roman Catholic Church for their differing beliefs in matters of the Holy Spirit, communion, and the ultimate authority of the pope.

It was on this topic that Thomas Aquinas began to write a lengthy treatise called *Against the Errors of the Greeks*. One could consider it perhaps a faux pas to think that you could convince anyone of anything simply by telling them that they are wrong, but the pope apparently felt that the work was substantial enough that it might work. Rather than beat around the bush, Aquinas was of the mind to tackle such ideological squabbles head-on. Even though at first glance some of his arguments may have seemed a bit aggressive in their bent to undermine his opponents, he always did so with love rather than avarice.

Much of the time, even his most ardent of challengers couldn't help but be taken with the passion and conviction with which Aquinas laid out his arguments. For most, it never seemed that Aquinas was simply trying to prove the other side wrong; it was just his deep-felt compassion for others that led him to pull him over to what he believed to be right. Thomas Aquinas was ever the zealous intellectual proselytizer, and in the church's greatest struggle between east and west, his talents and no-holds-barred approach were deemed to be necessary. If anyone could bridge the gap between the Roman Catholic Church and the Orthodox Catholic Church, it was believed that Thomas Aquinas could. It was a role that he seemed born to fulfill. As such, he quickly had the finished copy sent off to Michael Palaeologus, the current emperor of the Greek-speaking Byzantine Empire.

Thomas Aquinas's next trip abroad would be to London, England, in 1263. Not a whole lot is known about what transpired during this visit, but it is said that he was able to draw large crowds as was usually the case with his theological lectures. A total of some 300 were present to hear Thomas Aquinas speak. Furthermore, it is recounted that the King Henry III of England was among those present, and in order to show his esteem to Aquinas and the order, he handed out new priestly robes to all the monks present.

Right around this time, the Vatican was rocked by changes once again in the form of the sudden passing of Pope Urban IV in 1264 and the election of Pope Clement IV. This new pope, like the one that came before him, thought rather highly of Thomas Aquinas—so much so in fact that he nominated him to become the archbishop of Naples. Aquinas decided not to accept this prestigious position, however, and continued to teach in cities such as Bologna and Paris. During the following years, he also worked diligently on his unfinished books and wrote a plethora of treatises. Many years would pass before Aquinas finally returned to Naples.

Arriving in Naples in 1272, Aquinas set up his own university, enlisting handpicked faculty to teach new recruits of the Dominican order. Although he was quite busy in the lecture circuit at Naples, he still found time to continue working on what would become his most famous work, *Summa theologiae*. Now in his late forties, Thomas Aquinas was in his intellectual prime.

Chapter Nine

Late Life and Death

"Better to illuminate than merely to shine, to deliver to others contemplated truths than merely to contemplate."

—Thomas Aquinas

As soon as Thomas Aquinas made his new home in Naples, he was visited by several notables who sought his advice. Among these visits was a rather notable one with the cardinal legate of the Holy See and the bishop of Capua. With these men, Aquinas discussed at length all manner of theological difficulties.

When Thomas wasn't engaged in discussion, he was usually writing. He would finish up several more works during his stay at Naples, as well as adding to his *Summa theologiae*. What was remembered more than anything else, however, were Aquinas's continued, alleged supernatural encounters. As later dictated by his secretary, Aquinas was found on one occasion to be in animated conversation in the middle of the night. No one was in his room with him, but people could hear Aquinas's voice engaged in a heated debate with an unknown presence.

Once the conversation had ended, Aquinas quickly alerted his secretary, "Light the lamp!" The secretary then dutifully lit a lamp and brought it over to him. In the illumination, it could be seen that he was indeed by himself. Aquinas contended that just moments before, he was visited by a presence who instructed him to write. To the amazement of his secretary, Aquinas then began to vigorously write a complex treatise as it if had just been dictated to him from beyond. Wishing to know where the source of his inspiration had come from, the bewildered secretary is said to have thrown himself down before Aquinas and pleaded with him that he reveal who it was that he had been speaking to just a few moments prior.

Initially, Aquinas demurred, "It little befits you to know." But the secretary was insistent and continued to beg for him to reveal his source, crying out, "In the name of God, give me this little proof of friendship." Apparently unable to resist an order given with such conviction, Aquinas finally relented. He informed his faithful secretary that it was none other than the Apostles Paul and Peter who had dropped down from heaven to speak with him. As his amazed secretary took this information in, Aquinas then added the caveat, "But in the name of God I command you not to breath a word of this to anyone during my lifetime." The astonished secretary apparently kept his promise and did indeed not mention the unusual experience until after Thomas Aquinas left this world.

Another even more interesting account is in regard to Aquinas allegedly seeing the spirit of a certain Dominican professor by the name of Father Romain, whom he had been acquainted with during his time in Paris. What makes this alleged encounter so remarkable is that Aquinas supposedly had this visitation with the spirit of the deceased man before word had reached Naples of his demise. Father Romain had apparently died just a few days before Aquinas's vision, and owing to the fact of how slow information traveled from city to city in those days, no one in Naples yet knew that he had died.

Yet before anyone else had any inkling of his passing, Aquinas reportedly came forward with his startling account of speaking with Father Romain's disembodied ghost. Romain allegedly reported to Aquinas that he had just spent a few days in purgatory and was now on his way to "the happiness of heaven." Aquinas's peers in Naples didn't know what to make of the strange account, but when a few days later they learned that Romain was dead, they were completely shocked at Aquinas's foreknowledge.

As dedicated as he had been for most of his life, in his later years, Aquinas drew even closer to his faith. He was said to frequently fall into bouts of religious ecstasy in which he was so focused on his exuberant prayers and praise that it was hard to snap him out of it or pull him away from his devotion. Nevertheless, in 1274, he had to momentarily take leave of his holy revelry when the pope had need of Aquinas's services.

The Vatican, long wanting to solve the problem of the great schism between the western Latin half of Christendom and the eastern Greek half, summoned Thomas Aquinas to a council meeting in Lyon, modern-day France, requesting him to bring his book on the Greek errors to help heal the rift between the two Catholic churches. Aquinas was much older now and not quite so accustomed to traveling as he used to be in his younger days, but nevertheless, he heeded the call of the pope and set off for his mission.

During the course of the journey, Aquinas apparently suffered a very nasty fall. As he was traveling down the road from Terracina, his mule passed under a broken tree branch hanging over the road. Aquinas was struck in the head by the branch, causing him to fall to the ground. It's not clear if he lost consciousness from the blow, but he was apparently so still that his companions feared he was dead. After a moment, he stirred, and his friends were able to revive him back to a well enough state to continue their journey.

From here, they arrived at the castle of Maenza in which Aquinas's niece Francesca and her husband Count Annibal de Ceccano lived. It was determined that they should pay Francesca and the count a visit. His traveling companions were perhaps hoping the rest would allow Aquinas enough breathing room to recuperate. To their great dismay, he only seemed to get worse. While he was accompanied by his kin at the dinner table, he grew faint and seemed to have no desire for food. Nevertheless, after a few days, Aquinas left for Rome on the back of his mule, hoping to complete his mission. It wasn't long before he fell ill once again and had to be taken to a monastery they came across along the way.

Arriving at the monastery of Fossanova on February 10, 1274, Aquinas once again sought rest, but instead of growing stronger from his bedrest, he only grew weaker. As it became clear that his life was leaving him, he gave a confession of his whole life and entreated the monks to allow him to take communion one last time. Shortly thereafter, on the morning of March 7, 1274, Thomas Aquinas passed away at age 49. He wasn't able to complete the immediate mission the pope had given him, but although this one temporal task had not been fulfilled, by the time of his passing he had completed much more than anyone had ever expected.

Chapter Ten

The Last Word of Aquinas

"Justice is a certain rectitude of mind whereby a man does what he ought to do in the circumstances confronting him."

—Thomas Aquinas

After his passing, Thomas Aquinas was placed in a state as if he were some kind of a fallen monarch. Indeed, to those that followed him in the Benedictine order, he would have seemed no less important of a figure, as was demonstrated in the attendance rolls on the day of his funeral service. Aquinas had a vast multitude attend his funeral—all wanted to hear the eulogy and last word of this great man of God.

If legend is to be believed, many miracles supposedly occurred during the funeral rites of Thomas Aquinas. Many claimed to have been cured of blindness, deafness, and even demon possession, just for being near the body of this deceased theologian. Aquinas no doubt would have been pleased because his very funeral seemed to be a spontaneous outburst of ecstatic joy, praise, and worship of God.

Nevertheless, just three short years after his passing, some of his old detractors re-emerged from the woodwork and began to criticize Thomas Aquinas anew. In their efforts, they requested and received condemnation for at least parts of the works of Thomas Aquinas through the auspices of Stephen Tempier, the bishop of Paris, and Robert Kilwardby, the archbishop of Canterbury, which went into effect in 1277.

The Dominican order was not about to abandon its beloved brother, however, and in 1279, they issued an official proclamation of their support for Thomas Aquinas. Here, the reputation of Aquinas stood between these two warring theological groups—his legacy hanging in the balance until on July 18, 1323, almost 50 years after his passing, Aquinas was canonized as a saint. Since Aquinas had managed to make it this far, there was no way the church was about to let a saint be disparaged any longer. The previous condemnations that had been leveled against Aquinas's work were ordered to be removed.

A couple of centuries later, on April 15, 1567, Thomas Aquinas was declared a Doctor of the Church—a rare distinction only given to those that are known to have contributed great theological works and God-inspired liturgy. Such titles had been given only a few times in the past, leaving Aquinas in great company with such epic writers as Saint Augustine and Saint Ambrose. He was indeed hoisted up onto the shoulders of giants, but the words that he wrote would carry him still further as his life and legacy continued to unfold several centuries after he had left his earthly, physical coil behind.

Even though he had failed to complete his final journey down the Appian way in 1274, the words of Saint Thomas Aquinas would continue to lead the faithful down the path of divine enlightenment for several more centuries to come.

Conclusion

Perhaps the greatest legacy of Thomas Aquinas was his inquisitive mind. He dared to make inquiries into matters that most of his contemporaries never dreamed of questioning. Trained in the logic of classical philosophers such as Aristotle, Aquinas was able to equip these complex inquiries with such bulletproof logic from beginning to end that it was hard for his detractors to tear them apart.

Thomas Aquinas was not just good at asking fundamental questions, but he was also a tremendous force of reason when it came to creating logical arguments. When he first came to the seminary in Cologne, his peers took his silence as stupidity and mocked him as being a "dumb ox." But as he sat in silence before them, little did they know the tremendous thoughts that were racing through Thomas Aquinas's mind. Within the recesses of his brain, he was sifting through the stuff of existence itself.

Thomas Aquinas longed for answers and claimed that he had found them. They came to him both in the form of logical reasoning and alleged divine visitation—and sometimes the latter circumvented his own logical treatises. In fact, on December 6, 1273, Aquinas was in the middle of finishing his *Summa theologiae*—one of his greatest works—when he claimed to have been intercepted by the divine. This supernatural experience caused him to drop his pen and declare, "The end of my labours has come. All that I have written appears to be as so much straw after the things that have been revealed to me." Like Albert Einstein's unfinished theory of everything, which sought to place all the laws of the universe into one convenient package, Thomas Aquinas too left his greatest work incomplete.

Although Aquinas passed away several centuries ago, his is a legacy that is still unfolding. The camps still seem divided as to whether he was a great theologian, an ingenious philosopher, or merely some sort of fortunate hack who was riding the coattails of prior thinkers that came before. But whatever people may think of the work of Thomas Aquinas, his life shines as a testament of utter faith and devotion.

Made in United States
Troutdale, OR
03/03/2025

29461893R00030